MAKING MARRIAGE WORK

MAKING MARRIAGE WORK

Meditations on 1 Corinthians 13

by

NORMAN W. GOODACRE

with cartoons by Noel Watson

THE CANTERBURY PRESS
NORWICH

Text © Norman W. Goodacre 1996
Cartoons © Alex Noel Watson 1996

First published 1996 by The Canterbury Press Norwich
(a publishing imprint of Hymns Ancient & Modern Limited,
a registered charity)
St Mary's Works, St Mary's Plain,
Norwich, Norfolk, NR3 3BH

British Library Cataloguing in Publication Data

A catalogue record for this book is available
from the British Library

ISBN 1-85311-129-5

*Typeset by David Gregson Associates
Beccles, Suffolk
and printed in Great Britain by
St Edmundsbury Press Limited
Bury St Edmunds, Suffolk*

DEDICATED
WITH LOVE AND AFFECTION TO
Margaret, Timothy, and Charles
who venture boldly along this way.

'For heaven's sake, Gloria, you're supposed
to go into marriage with your eyes open.'

CONTENTS

INTRODUCTION

The inspiration for these pieces is the 13th chapter of St Paul's first letter to the Corinthian Church – his essay on love. I have attempted to relate the seventeen verses to Christian marriage and titled the whole – *Making Marriage Work*.

Each piece begins with an aspect of love which leads into an issue of importance for today: cohabiting, contraception, violence, bearing grudges, forgiveness and so forth, and concludes with a suggestion for discussion.

The scene today in Christian marriage is not easy. Traditional marriages rub shoulders with cohabiting couples. Keen Christians come up against conflicting views. It remains important that Christian marriage should make a strong witness to the power and grace of God and to the strong supportive influence of the Church.

This monograph can be used as a basis for group discussion and study, or used personally as a guide to the achievement of a 'good marriage'. My hope is that it will help to 'Make Marriage Work'.

N.W.G.

1.   Love is Patient

The teacher had explained to her fifth form that a successful marriage was something you had to achieve. 'Oh no, Miss, not something else we have to work at', said one of the form. The comment reveals in a sentence the popular romantic view that when you fall in love the experience will carry you through to a successful marriage. Not so. The uniting of any two lovers is fraught with hazards: different people, different faiths and different backgrounds. Given the help that common interests and similar background brings there are still differing temperaments and expectations. And then there are always 'the relations'! The new title of the 'Marriage Guidance Council' is 'Relate' and this word indicates the importance of relationships. Almost every family has special interests and characteristics. Some are argumentative and pugilistic and others are quiet and scholarly. Get to know the family background. Cultivate them: not as an overwhelming phalanx, but as friends and supporters. Be patient. Today the child of a divorce may be brought up by grandparents almost exclusively. Children suffer considerably from divorce, but quite often benefits accrue and these should be discerned and valued; they may even exceed what the original parents might have been able to offer.

Whether marriage is of the common law kind or solemnised officially, it concerns two people and two different backgrounds. It is necessary to work out how you wish to be known and addressed, particularly by the young, who like 'uncles and aunts' and the elderly, tend to be traditional.

Contrary to popular belief, marriage does not concern only the husband and wife; it is a social institution as well as a personal relationship. Society is built on homes and families. Romance there is and always will be, as we saw in Edith Wharton's story of the Buccaneers, where the successful American business families decide to raid 'the old country' and marry titles and acquire stately homes. Predatory conquest, greed and vulgarity had temporary success but it all tended to end in scandal and disorder. Patient love combined with unselfishness is blessed by God.

Issue: **Confrontation**
Confrontation is useless as a method of discussion because you find that the bigger or stronger party uses force and there is an unequal fight. When two people want to discuss a problem a third party can be called in to act as an umpire to see 'fair play'. The stronger personality, the better talker, or even the more attractive partner, will tend to achieve victory but it matters that both partners are satisfied. Better to sit side by side and allow equal time and equal opportunity for points to be made. The important thing is for each person to *listen* and if necessary 'play back' the argument by expressing it differently or more simply. The aim of a discussion is to come to a mutual appreciation of two points of view. Toleration matters a lot.

Discuss: The value of arguing?

2.   Love is Kind

In marriage it is easy to be critical over background. We can be snobby, stand-offish or just simply 'out of tune'. Why has Coronation Street been such a successful soap over the years? Surely because the bonhomie in the Rovers Return has become a persistent factor of the life. We feel at home. And what is the important ingredient that makes this possible? A kindness that is willing to accept other people. Kindness to most people is a working of love and as such something to emulate. The background to a marriage is a sensitive area, something people have to come to terms with if success is to be achieved.

Susan Howatch in her Starbridge novels makes a good deal of this in her discernment of how origins, gifts, and ambitions interweave, to make outstanding characters like the Bishop and the Dean. What triumphs in the end is the good life and the

RICHARD & MARGARET
BANISTER
STILL BLISSFULLY
HAPPY AFTER
30 YEARS

opportunity for spiritual growth. Kindness makes a big contribution in this process.

It could be true to say that a marriage cannot easily founder if kindness is characteristic. There are two proverbs illuminating this: 'You have to be cruel to be kind', and 'Kindness kills'. There is illumination for marriage in both these sayings. Critical assessment is clearly necessary if people are to grow into maturity, and sometimes harsh treatment is vital for a character to be saved from deterioration and spiritual death.

Take a positive attitude to difficult and destructive family background: discern the problems and attempt to deal with them – drink, violence, ignorance, bigotry, an alien environment. Nothing is insoluble. Be realistic and get help if you can. Kindness attempts all this by stages: instead of sentimentality, kindness uses friendships, sympathy and understanding. All is grist to the mill. An open approach to the most recalcitrant of problems can achieve unexpected results. Solutions somehow come from great frustration and even betrayal. Kindness should persist.

Issue: **Sentimentality**

It is sentimental to use feelings too much. Always check against facts and good thinking. Bringing up a family involves a great deal of strong direction and firm teaching in the early days, and in the teens a lot of 'give and take'. Promises must be kept. Sometimes you have to be cruel to be kind. Kindness need not be sentimental but feelings remain important. Our aim in life should be to do what is *right* and not what we feel like doing.

Discuss: How important is it to be honest?

3. Love is Generous

I think it is rightly suggested that more marriages break up over money than sex. Today this truth is underlined because of the almost unconscious stress on making money. Of course money is a basic means of exchange. Money buys our homes and procures food, drink and services. It matters little whether it is a pound, a dollar or a yen or even the ecu promised when there is a European currency. We can express generosity in any kind of currency. Nor is it mainly a matter of who holds the purse strings. I favour strongly both partners – individually and together. The point at issue is simply the power that money exerts.

'Dad, is marriage politically correct?'

Ananias and Sapphira in the story recorded in Acts chapter 8 sold their goods as other Christians were doing, to give to the poor, but in their case they kept back some of the proceeds and suffered for so doing. A bit hard, you say. They justified the 'bending of the truth' but they were motivated by meanness. Good relationships founder in the same way. Greed and envy are sins. In a marriage both partners earn the money whether either or both have jobs. One or other may have the skill of management and should do just that. If both are to share equally, personal bank or building society accounts are essential so that each partner has independence; the common purse finances the mortgage, the car, the holidays and education. Neither partner has a 'right' to pry, but each has the unqualified privilege of equal sharing. This way mature confidence is built and personal gifts and expenditures can be made. If these get out of hand a further change in responsibility can be arranged. Money is a great sacrament of opportunity. Sometimes it is right to make an expensive gift for love, as the women who anointed Jesus did in the Pharisee's house. It is always good to give to those in need. Many people set aside a tenth of money gifts to give away and this can be undertaken personally or as a family. Generosity in marriage is a gift of love, and there are no better ways of exercising it than by the responsible use of money.

Issue: **Discipline**
To get to the top, to achieve success, and to aspire to a position of influence always requires discipline, particularly in money matters. This is not a popular idea but an important one if marriage is to be effective. Marriage requires effort and stickability. It should not be broken up without considerable effort and trial. Disciplines are essential. Can you budget? Can you be depended upon to fulfil an obligation? Can you discipline your generosity?

Discuss: Gifts and gestures

4. Love is Humble

Humility is not a popular virtue. 'God helps those who help themselves', it is said, and that that philosophy suits the English well. The one aspect of humility that does appeal is our dislike of boasting. The big 'I am' is recognised for what he or she is, very quickly, and shunned by those not involved in a 'Maxwell' type of money-making.

By way of contrast humility and love are the top virtues of the spiritual life. In marriage they speedily come into their own: instead of the hen-pecked husband you have the handy-man, and replacing the local gossip, the 'mother' in Israel. Humility makes all the difference. It is said that everyone loves a lover. Why is that? Love can be very selfish: a mutual admiration

'I thought I'd bring a little magic back into our marriage.'

society does not flourish. The secret of success is placing the other person first. The essence of humility is obedience to God and to circumstances, and humiliations show us the way. The real lover puts God first. A happy marriage does this. Sunday should claim our worship in the parish church or the church of our choice. There is no need to dress up. Husband and wife cannot always worship together unless there is a convenient crèche, but plans can be made. The point is to get the priorities right. Humility does this. 'Humble yourself under the mighty hand of God.'

The lowest place is the safest place. You are ready to serve as required. It is a relaxing place to be. There is no strain. Life in the office, the business, or the factory, can be very demanding. We come home to friendship and to support and relaxation. Welcome that. Home should be that kind of place. We all need sympathy and companionship. Home is the place to find them. Talking and listening, listening and talking. Love is humble exchange.

After a dusty and tiring day Jesus took a towel and girded himself to wash the disciples' feet. Not anything we should do here in the U.K., but essential in a hot climate. The disciples demurred. When I was a boy you never saw a pram being pushed by father, and you never saw men with children in their care. Today all this has changed for good. Both husband and wife can organise the family outing; both can minister to the children's needs because both can be humble enough to serve. Take the initiative: take the lower place.

Issue: **Cohabiting**
There may be a case for cohabiting before marriage if one of the parties is homosexual because sex is hard to sustain unless both are heterosexual. 'Trying it out' could show the dangers of a mixed homo and hetero marriage.

In heterosexual relations it is better to stick by the rules because it makes for the security of both partners (especially the woman) and it makes clear to the children who their relations are and how they are to be addressed. Society needs stability.

Where two homosexuals fall in love a blessing may be sought from God through the Church, but a marriage ceremony in my opinion is inappropriate.

Discuss: Security for women

5. Love is Appreciative

Appreciation is not easily given by people. Perhaps because to appreciate is to give part of yourself and that is always costly. Appreciation is very important, especially in marriage. It does, in fact, contribute to the well being of each partner. Honest, open, and whole-hearted recognition of worth and gifts is in itself a showing of God: It reflects the mystery and magic of creation and calls forth from us a desire to share in the joy. Blake understood this when he wrote these lines:

> He who bends to himself a Joy
> Doth the winged life destroy,
> But he who kisses the Joy as it flies
> Lives in Eternity's sunrise.

If we catch the vision we can share it with others. It is for this reason that we decorate and furnish our houses to make them attractive. And what wonders a garden can perform when its show is the admiration of the passers by.

There is everything to be said for telling your spouse, partner or friend that you love and appreciate him or her. This makes us all feel good. Better still perhaps, to provide a service, to remember the birthday and plan a romantic day out. My own parents were not of the demonstrative kind but I recall with delight that Mother saw Father off to the office each day with a wave from the door. At home he would give her a hug. My parents used few endearments as such, but their love and friendship was continuous, from walking home from school together right into old age. And all this in spite of Mother's shyness and dislike of the public life and her inability to join Father in many things he liked. They got the essentials right.

A word of appreciation to those outside the home circle is always welcomed though rarely given. Today the value of this is understood. A great friend who graduated with a first from university was never praised by her father and consequently never really learnt to value herself. He believed, for some odd reason, that praise would make his daughter big-headed when all she wanted was a recognition that her gifts and successes

were appreciated in the right quarter. It is a very important part of growing up into adult life that we should receive appreciation.

Issue: **Narcissism**

Do you contemplate your navel? Are you narcissistic? Some marriages and common law relationships are very inward looking, self-regarding mutual admiration societies. This can be escapist. Neighbours are neglected or ignored. Every type of society has its own social possibilities: middle class suburbia can be very friendly and mutually helpful without being in any way interfering. A working class community in Liverpool was strong enough to persuade the Council to re-house them 'on the site' where they had achieved a lively fellowship and good relationships. This Eldonian Community, next door to the original Tate and Lyle sugar factory in Liverpool, became a model pattern for similar experiments elsewhere. Neighbourliness is the opposite of narcissism.

Discuss: A 'mutual admiration society'

6. Love is Never Rude

Gentleness would not be immediately linked with sex in most people's minds. Gentleness conjures up a world of ease and comfort: people who are not normally rude; a world of leisure, good manners, and peace. My mind goes back to an occasion in the dinner hour at school when I was returning home for the mid-day meal and I was passed by one of the 'rougher' boys whom I knew. As he passed he called out a single expletive – no further comment. I knew the boy and something of his background, and I think it was natural for him, but the shock has remained with me for more than seventy years. Love is never rude: its usual and normal working is motivated by reverence.

A combination of fear and sex challenges normal loving and upsets people. Fears feed on ignorance, greed and curiosity. Information and education in sex are vital for the young. Curiosity can be met today through books, tapes and videos. To fail in this is to be a bad parent. Youth rightly needs information, and easily becomes impatient to know whether sexual orientation is hetero or homo. Self-knowledge leads to fulfilment. Heterosexual sex means that it is natural to cleave to the opposite sex for fulfilment; homosexual interest centres on the same sex. The former is more usual but both can be used by God. Observation makes it clear that some of the greatest artists, priests and actors are homosexual and their influence considerable, especially amongst their own sex.

Gentleness is a quality of love that commends itself in all personal dealings and especially in sexual relationships. Good foreplay can greatly increase the delight in making love. Sex is natural whereas rudeness is boorish. We need all the help we can get when we are learning the art of intimate relationships. We shall often need to 'try again', to 'do better', and to 'persevere': reverence rather than rudeness helps.

Issue: **Good Manners**

It was my good fortune to meet a senior couple who had little in common and whose marriage was generally considered to be a 'mistake'. This marriage was saved by 'good manners'. This meant that in speaking to one another and reacting to each other, courtesy was always observed. The result was the kind of situation one hopes that Prince Charles and Princess Diana might achieve when the throne is reached and the children are 'in line'. The solution may be painful, but very necessary and much better for the family.

Discuss: Does swearing help or hinder?

'You mean they lived happily ever after without
seeing a marriage counsellor?'

7. Love is altruistic

The word altruism has overtones of the impersonal: the Oxford dictionary defines it as 'regard for others'; not exactly a characteristic of lovers though the intention is often there. A great deal of splendid work is done in the world by altruism. It is said that America is run by women over the age of sixty who have brought up their families and are now free to 'run the country', and very successfully they do it too. Love is never selfish says St Paul. Unfortunately, we are all very selfish by nature. Only the grace of God can work the miracle. Most people like to do it 'their way'.

'You vandal! You've damaged the tree!'

Here is a good recipe for two people setting up home together, in a town or village where they are not known: smile and be friendly, and listen to all advice on offer; be ready to ask for information and help whenever it is needed. Keep a low profile. Introduce yourselves quietly. Support the neighbours by being ready to 'feed the cat' or take in the post. Whatever you may feel about 'other people' bear in mind that we all need neighbours and it's good to have them on your side.

It could be said that suburbia thrives on altruism. In a given area there are gurus who are experts in almost everything; they delight to be approached in their garden sheds, garages and greenhouses. There will always be some who like to keep themselves to themselves and their wishes have to be respected. Most of us need neighbours. New estates may seem 'unfriendly' but it is only a veneer. Feel your way. True altruism has to present a slightly impersonal attitude so that none are offended. It takes time to break down barriers of class, breeding and snobbery, but these can all be replaced by the virtue of friendship. Christian love expresses itself well in altruism.

Issue: **Having a Faith**
People today think that they have outgrown religion and can manage without it. Never could they be more mistaken. Many give up their childhood faith because it never 'grew up' and instead have taken up with astrology and read their horoscopes. This is nonsensical in today's scientific world. It is of secondary importance which particular faith you take up; what does matter is that you follow something good. Life is centred in God and it is important to make the right choices with his help.

Worship is an essential element in human life. We all have to worship something or somebody, even if it is only ourselves! The pop star, the T.V. idol, the sporting hero or heroine, all claim their worshippers. But where are the counsellors and the friends? Church or Chapel provide these helpers and problems can be taken there.

Discuss: 'Getting too caught up'

15

8. Love is not given to taking Offence

No better commendation for success in life could be made than a determination not to take offence. We seem to live in a world of litigation today: professional people – doctors, journalists, public leaders all fear the law, and at the same time are quick to leap into the solicitor's office on their own behalf. It is not a relaxing existence having a law suit hanging over you. It tends to shorten life rather than make it more worth while. How much better to apologise or explain, and get things put right. St Paul asks in his letter to Corinth: 'Why go to law before the pagan court when you could settle "before God's people"?' (1 Cor 6.1) 'Out of Court'.

Love is not given to taking offence. Love is forgiving. The intimacy of marriage offers limitless opportunities for 'putting things right'. Backgrounds vary – some dominate. 'We always went abroad for our holidays'. 'We always kept Christmas this way'. The first decade of marriage tends to be an opportunity for testing backgrounds. Fortunately most people today understand something of psychology and recognise why they like to lie in on Sundays and read the papers, or wash the car on Sunday mornings just when the Christian couple will be wondering about worship and its claim on their weekend. Women are very often sympathetic over background while men tend to regress into childhood and 'play' with trains, or hobbies. Characters like Fred Dibnah, the steeplejack from Bolton, and steam buffs, are so dyed in the wool that a new wife becomes a 'necessity' to find peace. Christian spouses and partners have to put up with these things or come to some arrangement so that life can go on. The important thing is to play fair. 'There's nowt so queer as folks', so says the old Yorkshire jibe.

In all the vagaries of coming to terms with human nature it has to be remembered that it is important to take action. It is all very well not wanting to take offence, but peace comes to those who make a workable plan. This is the secret of the lasting success of the T.V. series *Last of the Summer Wine*. Three quite incompatible characters get along in a splendid and amusing way because they each insist on doing their own thing. That is why arranged marriages, so despised by the English temperament, can often be extremely successful because those advising are old enough to know what two people need.

Issue: **Forgiveness**

Nothing is harder than forgiveness, yet nothing is more important. Until the Japanese nation acknowledges the wickedness of their prisoner of war camps and make apology and recompense it will be difficult to restore relationships. The same need for forgiveness is experienced in Anglo-Irish relationships as these too await mutual confession and forgiveness before life can move forward happily and creatively once again. Exactly the same thing is to be recognised in *personal* relationships: individual hatreds and fears have to be faced and exorcised. Ask your priest, guru or counsellor how to do it.

Discuss: Blaming the family or the neighbours.

9.   Love keeps no score of Wrongs

They say the elephant never forgets. Some cultures and some people are very retentive of hurts sustained over the years. When the Vicar of St James, Piccadilly, invited representatives of the Anglican and Roman churches to give Lenten addresses on the differences and clashes in their mutual backgrounds it was possible to see, perhaps for the first time, what terrible things Christians do to one another in pursuance of what each side believes to be right. These meetings became occasions for confession, shame and the determination to 'do better'. It is necessary for great sin to be recognised for what it is and how it crucifies God. In this way alone can we hope for resurrection and new life? We have to start all over again with our loving, because 'love keeps no score of wrongs'. Forgiveness is available. New life lies just ahead. This is the meaning of the word to Mary Magdalene in the Garden of the Resurrection when Jesus simply said, 'Mary'. No resentment, no blame, no recriminations. Simply an instruction: 'Go to my brothers and tell them.'

It is easy in a close relationship like marriage to keep a secret list of wrongs and upsets which should have been dealt with immediately. A score of misunderstandings is dangerous. It leads to a memory filled with recrimination when explanations should have been uttered.

We must set ourselves more workable standards for the future. The clearness of the problem as we see it individually, may make it necessary to consult a friend, or Relate, or the local church and minister.

Very often it is the 'clown' or the 'fool' who does best because he or she can sense the sadnesses and absurdities in life and begin to laugh at themselves. We have to forget pride, pick ourselves up and start afresh. We need forgiveness and it is available directly from God or through the Church.

Issue: **Holding a Grudge**

Learning to love is difficult especially when we hold fast to a grudge. Examining such a situation usually reveals a deep-seated hatred or misunderstanding – some rebuff of many years ago, a prejudice or a fear. The Christian cannot take this way out of a problem. Grudges must be removed. A solution has to be found although it will go against the grain. Grasp this nettle and act quickly. Help may be obtained from local Christian Fellowships, or from Relate, the Marriage Guidance Council. Psychological help can be sought and found in the Clinical Theology field which Frank Lake initiated in Nottingham in the middle of this century. You can approach them through your own diocesan centre or office.

Discuss: Going to Law – right or wrong?

'Of course, ours will be a non-smoking marriage!'

19

10. Love takes no pleasure in the Sins of Others

The Sunday newspapers delight in the sins of others. It is a cynical comment that the English enjoy their sex at second hand by reading all about it in the papers, or for that matter in the 'modern novel'. If we defend this attitude by saying people desire to have their 'affairs' publicised, the 'editors' certainly love to have it so. They aid and abet. They know when they are on to a good thing. It takes a strong minded believer not to guzzle from this trough. The justification for requiring salacious information is in order to heal or to fight a cause.

It is altogether good to support people in trouble; to find occasions for praise and appreciation rather than criticism. It is one of the faults of a close relationship that continuous grumbling and criticism can ruin lives. 'Getting out of bed on the wrong side' is an excuse for bad feelings, though this is hardly a possible excuse if you occupy the same bed! What is needed is a morning cup of tea. The traditional English breakfast is often consumed behind the paper, or dominated by the T.V. or radio. I always feel very sorry for those who are obliged to 'have breakfast with Frost'. Emergencies are different, when we need to know what is going on. I am often surprised by the way people bully themselves over getting off to work. Lack of planning and organisation and a rush for the train can be replaced by a pleasant walk to the bus or by starting earlier. And then there are those couples who put up with overwork, coming home late and losing precious time together. Bringing work to do at home is not worth the extra cash. The strain can be deadly. Togetherness is vital in a marriage, even if it is simply quiet reading in the evening. Life can be marked by special events. There can be more fun in a lunch or snack at the 'local' with a baked potato than the long wait for service when you go out to what is reputed to be a good restaurant! Food is important but relationships by the staff who produce it often counts for more.

Friends are there to be visited but need not overwhelm with bonhomie. The English are a shy race and have to be girded up to 'do the honours'. Scatter such visits and enjoy them all the more. And whenever you and your spouse have a common hobby – fell-walking, pub-visiting or architectural photography or whatever – make the most of it. We have elderly friends in Iowa in the USA – busy farmers who look forward to a winter session of country dancing in the local town. When you have things to enjoy there is less time for criticism and more for fun.

Issue: **The Tabloid Press**

You may read the Tabloids and maybe you like these popular papers. Perhaps you take your political or even your religious views from their content. Bear in mind that the popular press lives by its success in recording a good deal of sleaze. Unfortunately human nature finds it very hard to avoid complicity with evil and many of us read the salacious, the critical

and the censorious because it makes us feel good. Bear this in mind and maintain your critical faculties. Don't believe all you read in the papers. Remember that as a Christian you have to stand up for what is right and good and be ready to challenge the popular and sexy.

Discuss: Crime, unemployment and drugs

11. There is nothing Love will not face

Not being of a courageous disposition myself I always admire those who attain to such heights. They are the V.C. types who often come from very unexpected backgrounds. I had absolutely no sympathy at all for the boys at school who used to dare their peers to do this and that which was clearly dangerous and foolish. In fact I scorned that approach to life and tended to write off those who indulged. The 'show-off' is never a very popular character though he or she can always attract a crowd. Their feats have overtones of courage but lack common sense.

Courage in adult life rightly attracts great admiration. Of course there are many absurdities as shown in the Guinness Book of Records, but outstanding courage is to be seen more clearly in those who have faced accident, bereavement, brutal attack, and medical bad news bravely. The good parish priest meets a lot of such people and they illuminate a church. Such challenges call out the best in us all. Examples are everywhere: the husband who cares for the children, the wife who copes with drink in the family; the 'black sheep' and the feckless neighbour. They all have to be helped. The acceptance of a killing cancer, the refusal to let accident or misfortune sour relationships; the courageous facing up to a mistaken judgment, the loss of promotion prospects in business or sheer 'bad luck'. All these require great courage to cope with and, when accepted, make a marriage as strong as a rock.

Although it tends towards the sentimental and is geared to romantic youth, I have always liked the Knight's Prayer. I met it first when visiting an Art Gallery and I immediately wrote it down. Here it is:

> 'My Lord, I am ready on the threshold of this new day to go forth armed with your power, seeking adventure on the highroad, to right wrong, to overcome evil, to suffer wounds and endure pain if need be, but in all things to serve you bravely, faithfully and joyfully so that at the end of the day's labour, kneeling for your blessing, you may find no blot upon my shield.'

Issue: **Adultery**

The reason why adultery is such a powerful 'turn-off' in marriage is quite simply because it sins against the intimacy of making love in the safe context of Christian marriage (see the Castles' series on BBC1 Summer 1995). Adultery was the original reason for divorce, but that was in the days before people realised how serious it is to break up a marriage – what harm it does to the partners and to their children. Today, fortunately, we are coming to realise that serious though it is, adultery is not the 'end'. Forgiveness can and should be exercised and an honest talking through the problems should be undertaken under the guidance of God the Holy Spirit.

Discuss: Is this the last straw?

12. Love has no Limits

It is said that forty is the most dangerous age for a husband when he can be tempted to look around at other women. The predatory and hunting male, even in a stable marriage will cast his eye around. If he happens to be vulnerable in this direction he needs to rehearse the teaching of the Sermon on the Mount and take a firm stand for the right and the good. To do otherwise is to jeopardise something precious which he has valued up to now. To lose a marriage for a passing temptation is foolishness indeed. Whichever partner is suffering temptation something can always be done. What should it be? Perhaps this is the moment for a holiday of a lifetime, or a change of house. Maybe you just take your courage in both hands and consult a counsellor. Love is strong enough to cover all emergencies, but action must be taken. You may be absolutely certain that you could successfully overcome a temptation to break up a marriage, but beware. There is danger. The middle years are famous

'Darling, I'm calling upon all your love and understanding ...'

for self-delusion; you can be blind and dumb. There will be elements in the situation where you can exercise skill and sympathy. Love has no limits. If you are spiritually minded, take a quiet day, go on a retreat, make your confession.

Remember that the devil dislikes a 'face to face' approach. Challenge him. Make fun of him. Laugh at him and at yourself! You will be surprised how things will suddenly change and you will find yourself on the straight and narrow once more. The devil thinks he can get away with it. You know better. Say that word. Do that kind deed. Make that right choice and offer the whole thing to God. In a marriage mutual togetherness offers plenty of opportunities for discussion and facing up to dangers. Be courageous. Love is very strong. God is on your side. Extend your observation and try to look around and see what is going on. The middle years tend to be a time of sitting back and being satisfied. This is fatal. Self-absorption is self-destructive. Say the word. Do the right thing. Consult Relate (for address see section 16).

Issue: **Test-tube babies**
Test-tube babies do not exactly suggest love, though concerned partners may very well be unable to conceive a child in any other way. Love in that case surrounds the test-tube which after all is simply a means of bringing a new life into the world. What matters in that case is the fulfilment of a hope for the couple in question. There are clearly permutations and combinations that are not Christian at all. The possibility of a scientifically cloned society for evil purposes is clearly a danger and a blasphemy. So let us not 'throw out the baby with the bath water'.

Discuss: Setting limits

13. Love is always Hopeful

It was always recognised that violence disrupted marriage and the earliest form of divorce was separation. Those who are unable to control temper become a menace to themselves as well as to others, and just as society has organised 'drying out' for dipsomania, so we are needing today a retraining for uncontrollable anger. The vocal hurl expletives and the less vocal resort to violence as a quick and easy way of indicating their views. Clearly this kind of mass hysteria lies behind tribal problems in Africa. It is the same with the clash between the British and Irish attitudes to life. It is seen in terms of personal one to one relationships when two people refuse to speak to one another and an impasse is created which requires a solution, through the mediation of friends and counsellors. Violence can be diffused this way, but in the long term retraining is required as the basic clash of personality is very deep.

In setting about dealing with this it has to be recognised that we are working against fear. It can be as dangerous as joining a street fight. This is the hell which violence makes for people. It can end in marriage break-up, chronic illness, prostrating inhibition and an escape into what is only a half-life in a refuge. What can we offer to those who face these problems and who do not approach their local church or social group? It is all very negative and difficult, but if we remember that God and the infinite power of good is on our side, then we can go forward with trust, and the wisdom of friends and supporting groups will help. Do not go it alone. Remember that the violent person is also running away from his or her own life and that fear lies behind most violent people. We must be hopeful.

Once again we need to learn that marriage is not just a two-person relationship: it concerns society, through relations and friends. We need not wait for the first trauma, the mugging, the fight, the burglary or the accident, to learn that we need help. Friends there are if we look for them, and although the law is not inclined to enter into domestic quarrels, family and friends can do what the law cannot. Go forward with God and you will find a way through to peace.

Issue: **Violence**

The popular press reports violence because it is startling and promotes fear. Violence is the weak man or woman's escape from the frustrations of pride and jealousy. It is exacerbated by anger and very often issues in 'grievous bodily harm'. These traumas exist at all levels of society and help is needed everywhere. We need time to calm down, restore peace and undertake counselling. 'Count ten', we used to say as children. There are always better ways of solving problems than going to war, and that is what violence does. Once again find out where you can turn for help. Healing, through counselling, confession and forgiveness, *is* available and should be sought and used.

Discuss: Temperamental tantrums

14. Love Suffers and Endures

There are plenty of perks in being married; a close friendship supported by a sexual relationship which can be good, bad, or indifferent, but is always worth working at. The art of loving is very important and can be improved. On the other hand marriage has its chores and these too should be studied and made obedient to a joint working philosophy. It was always our custom for every member of the family, and all guests, to join in the washing up after a good meal. We did a lot of family chat during all this and indeed we got rid of the dishwasher in order to be able to hear each other speak!

The shock of bad news; the loss of money or job; misunderstandings and jealousies, can all play havoc in a marriage. When there is a major setback we shall find that life goes deeper and means more. We emerge from a trauma with additional courage and stature. Love suffers and endures.

Discovering signposts in life is important. I am not talking about superstition or bad luck; I mean discerning the leading of God. The normal approach to life should include looking for the working of God in day-to-day activity. God is always there, whether we recognise him or not. Nor does he support only those who pray. God is love and for this reason he is always indicating the right way ahead, pointing out the dangers. He makes clear the general pattern which we should follow.

My opposite neighbour drives a taxi at night: not the easiest of jobs and one which very often seems to involve him in a very thorough cleaning of his car the following day. This good taxi driver, like the good publican, is a source of support and a signpost to the self-centred when drink is about.

There are few better ways of suffering and enduring to good effect on life today than the testimonies of such men and women. Love suffers and endures: let the newly weds and married couples copy.

Issue: **The George Cross**

I've always thought that the G.C. is even more appropriate for valour than the V.C. because it is a civil life award. Many marriages qualify for this kind of 'gong' because despite problems of temperament, heredity, drink, drugs, and sheer bloody-mindedness they survive and inspire. Most of us could name half a dozen marriages where the courageous behaviour of the partners against great odds qualifies them for a G.C.; illness, tragedy, bad luck, financial loss, not to mention unemployment, are some of these things.

Discuss: Can love disappear?

'Marriage may be a lottery, but mine is certainly up to scratch.'

15. Love is Faithful

Faith is essential in any life. Without it we would not even cross the road. In marriage it is important at the beginning and it goes right on to the end. Children are not always born when expected or wanted, so you may be caught out over dates. I know a family where birthdays are spread out over eight months of the year, and I know families where birthdays are at Christmas when it becomes important to arrange a 'royal birthday' in June.

Sharing news and views between partners can be a vital part of a good marriage. I think partners are missed more for this than for almost anything else. Where love and faith meet in this family relationship there is great strength and unity. Faith takes various forms in marriage. You set out with the idea of a nuclear family and you find you have four or even six children. I know a lonely wife on a farm in the vastness of the American heartland where they had a family of eight almost without realising it. But if you have no children what do you do? I must testify that in a long life I have known of many very successful adoptions: children need parents and married couples normally delight in children. You can put the two together and make happiness. You may hope to continue the family line in Victorian style. I know of a family who set out to do just that and had eleven children, all of whom were girls except the middle child who when adult did not marry. 'The best laid schemes ...' as the poet Burns said.

Sensible people accept what God gives, but they also use their own ideas and hope. Factors like health, money, gifts, and ambition, all play their part. Love is faithful. By faith we move forward steadily and in old age when we look back we shall discern the leading of God and find that 'all has been well'. In Pilgrim's Progress, John Bunyan has Faithful accompanying Christian as he comes to the 'river of death' and crosses over on to the other side. The Heavenly City welcome Faithful as it welcomes Christian.

Issue: **Birth Control**
It is difficult to understand why Rome is against birth-control, except by what is called the natural method. I think it is largely a fear of losing control. A male-orientated church finds it difficult to see the problem from the woman's point of view. When Romes comes round to a common leadership of men and women things will immediately improve. The spirit of Pope John 23 is still abroad and his 'honest to God' kind of approach will continue to exercise a good Christian influence.

Discuss: Abortion

16. Love in Community

In the Bible Reading Fellowship notes on Acts 15, 12–21 in 1995, the writer says 'The strict sexual teaching which Christianity inherited from Judaism proved vital. Marriage and family life were very unstable in the Roman world; wives were often abandoned to live in lonely poverty, and children received little care and affection. But the Christian Church soon gained a high reputation for the unity and happiness which Christian married couples enjoyed, and for the love which children received both from their parents and from other Christian adults. Christian men were sometimes mocked for their lack of sexual adventure, but more often Christian families were admired, even envied, by others and this was a major factor in drawing people towards the Faith.' May it long continue!

'So marriages <u>are</u> made in Heaven!'

The attraction of life in a Christian community is powerful for building up the Faith. It is seen working in the Christian Church where Baptism, Confirmation and Holy Communion sustain and where Sunday worship includes time for social meeting and teaching sessions. This presents the opportunity for a Christian Family Life which sustains marriage and education in personal relationships very satisfactorily.

For love in community to prosper we need the provision of Advice Bureaux, Counselling Training, and Religious Education Study so that new people coming into the Church can use these helps and benefit from them. The following address may be useful to those who wish to explore Relate.

Relate (Marriage Guidance Counselling)
Herbert Gray College
Little Church Street
RUGBY CV21 3AP
Telephone 01788 573241

Issue: **Divorce**
There is great power in societies where marriages are strong and based on Christian love. Many political and social writers have seen the truth of this stability where it can be achieved. Divorce is a canker in society. It is a confession of failure. Broken homes mean separated families, shortage of housing, cramped conditions, with that underlying anxiety about the 'purpose of God in the life of the world'. Faith, hope, and charity remain the three vitally important virtues, but they very easily fly out of the window when divorce is in the air. Christian love means a settled family life in a settled community where the family can find security and opportunity for growth.

Discuss: Does divorce matter to others?

17. Love is the Only Way

We have looked at Christian Marriage in these pieces and come to the conclusion that love is the only way. Sex is central without being dominant. Love is recognisable in a thousand different ways – all important, while selfishness spoils and creates havoc. The model for success is a recognition that God has priority and that obedience to Christian law is fundamental. Models for success are to be found in good home life, co-operation of husband and wife and welcome for the family. Disaster attends the egotist, and disappointment the salacious. Recognition of the importance of each individual person opens the way to an achievement of wholeness in the home.

Love can be found both in success and in failure because it blossoms in adversity and achieves its highest renown in situations on course for disaster. Nothing is impossible where love is at work. When we are tempted to despair, spurned and crucified by events over which we seem to have little control then that is the very moment for a new act of faith in God and a new effort. This way an endangered marriage can come together again. We can experience resurrection and new life. The twin virtues of love and humility in any marriage become the essential ingredients of success. It was Jesus himself who recommended taking the lowest place and being beneath everyone, and Jesus too who said that 'greater love hath no man than this: that he lay down his life for his friends'. No wonder that successful marriages turn on their ability to copy and demonstrate these virtues.

Thanks be to you, my Lord Jesus Christ,
For all the benefits you have won for me,
For all the pains and insults you have borne for me,
Most merciful Redeemer, Friend, and Brother,
May I know you more clearly,
Love you more dearly,
And follow you more nearly,
day by day.

St Richard of Chichester

Issue: **Success**

Where should we look for success? First of all in a good working friendship between husband and wife – between devoted partners. A sacramental life where gifts are shared and appreciated and where opportunities and problems are faced openly by the whole family. Of course every home will experience problems as well as success and this should be expected and embraced. In the Christian Church Holy Week and Good Friday are followed by Holy Saturday and Easter Day. God blesses the humble and the clever: he gives support to the foolish as well as to the wise, and he directs us all into a fullness that comes to Christian marriage and Christian community. We are never alone. God is always there and we may always rely on his loving care and direction until we find our final destiny in Heaven.

Discuss: The redeeming power of love

'I'm sorry, darling, this isn't really much of a second honeymoon.'